Reader's
Digest

# How to
# Trace Your
# Family History
# on the Internet

PUBLISHED BY THE READER'S DIGEST ASSOCIATION, INC.
LONDON • NEW YORK • SYDNEY • MONTREAL

# Contents

## First steps 10

Before you launch into the adventure of family history, it pays to do some groundwork. This chapter introduces you to the best family history websites, sets out the basics of family history research and then looks in more depth at what's online and where to start. You'll see the types of documents you should collect, and learn how to get the best out of your PC as your research progresses.

## Building your family tree 66

Now it's time to turn detective and discover your ancestors – the building blocks for your family tree. You'll see how to work online with the key web resources – indexes to births, marriages and deaths, census returns, parish register indexes and wills. You'll then learn how to identify ancestors from old documents and how to work back through the generations to find those early forebears.

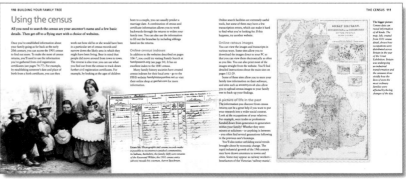

## Your family's story 176

Once you've discovered who your ancestors are, you can start to bring them to life. You'll learn about how they lived day-to-day, their homes, work and hobbies, and the society to which they belonged. Using online resources you can find out about your ancestors' occupations, military service and their travels, including immigration and emigration – and even if they broke the law.

## Making contact 262

When you've gathered all the information about your family, you'll probably want others to enjoy it as well. This chapter shows you how to use the internet as a tool for sharing discoveries with your immediate and extended families. Case histories will help you to trace living relatives and show you how to put your own discoveries online, including photographs, documents and family trees.

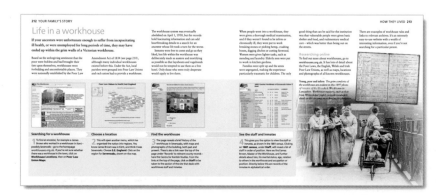

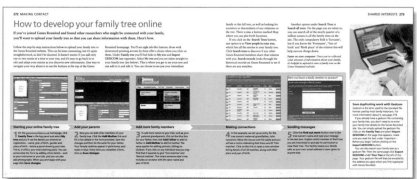

# About this book

**Although you're probably itching to get started on your family history, it's a good idea to browse right through the book first, to get an overall view of what it contains, what the possibilities are and consider how far you want to go in the search for your ancestors.**

Once you've decided what area of your family you want to research, you're ready to start making your first steps, guided on your journey by the pages of this book. You may be content simply to create a family tree for you and your immediate family to enjoy. Or maybe you have grander ideas and plan to share your findings with far-flung family members, get involved with family-tree sharing websites or even start your own blog or forum. Be prepared for surprises – you may become so absorbed by your researches that you find your initially modest plans transformed into something more ambitious.

## What you'll find in the book

*How to Trace Your Family History on the Internet* is divided into four chapters – First steps, Building your family tree, Your family's story and Making contact (see pages 4-5 for more detail). They introduce you to family history, show you how to build a family tree, help you to find out what sort of people your ancestors were and suggest ways of making contact with your wider family.

At the back of the book, as well as the index, you'll find a 'Directory' with addresses, phone numbers and websites for all the information sources mentioned in the text, as well as other bodies that may help you to take your research even further.

50 FIRST STEPS

## Using online data services
## ancestry.co.uk

A number of key websites, including Ancestry, offer vast amounts of information – your ancestors will be in there somewhere. You may have to pay for the information, but it's well worth it.

Some of the information on Ancestry is free – for example, the birth, marriage and death indexes for England and Wales. You can search these indexes by clicking the **Family Trees** link near the top of the homepage. But to access most of the data collections you'll need either to

**Ancestry records include:**

- UK censuses (1841-1911)
- Birth, marriage and death indexes for England and Wales (1837-2005)
- Parish and probate records (1538-1980)
- British Army WW1 service records (1914-20)
- London Metropolitan Archives
- Pallot's Marriage Index for England (1780-1837)
- UK Incoming Passenger Lists (1878-1960)

take out a subscription (wh... access to all the records wit... payment) or use the pay-pe... where you pay for a fixed n... searches. Whichever you ch... by credit card and your sub... renewed automatically unle...

There are separate UK a... subscriptions, but unless y... Ancestry has records for a c... ancestors came from or we... membership should cover a...

**What's in the index...**
Take a look at the yellow b... see what information is hel... site. Like most other data s... relatively little material for... of which is available only o... (see page 56).

Ancestry has an enormo... different datasets, and in m... provide not only an index a... of the records but also imag... records. This means you ca... for yourself, to check again... given in the index.

**Seeing the images**
To display these images, A... special image viewer with f... printing and zooming. On... image on your own compu... or print it as you need.

In addition to the basic i... Ancestry also has an Enhan... which provides a wider ran... including a facility for mag...

**Go to the homepage**

**1** The design of the ancestry.co.uk homepage changes often, but it always gives you details of the records on offer. The tabs at the top provide further information about what you can do on the site. Access is via a registration and subscription service, but you can usually have a free 14 day trial. To register as a member, click on **Subscribe** on the top right-hand side of the page.

**Register and subscribe**

**2** On the registration page you'll be asked to select an annual or monthly membership package. There are three different packages available: The basic subscription (**Essentials**) is sufficient for most uses; you'll want the **Premium** subscription if want to view military records; and **Worldwide** if you think your ancestry stretches beyond the UK. There are also pay-per-view options available. Select your preferred plan and click on **Become a member**.

**Give your details**

**3** Enter your name and email address and click on **Continue**. This takes you to another page where you enter your contact details. Then enter your credit card details. Make sure you read and accept the terms and conditions of the site. Once you're registered, you have access to the records via a series of search screens.

**Following the steps** Throughout the book, case histories are used to show you how to make the most of websites and family history software. These examples appear in a coloured band running across a page or spread, with each step clearly titled and numbered. The step text includes simple instructions, giving you the links you need to follow (with just a click of your mouse) marked in **bold type**. Above each step is an image of what you'll see on screen during the process – you'll simply need to insert your own family search details or requests at these points. Where the book shows screens from downloaded software, don't worry if the borders and buttons look a little different on your PC – this should not affect any instructions the book gives you.

**Websites** Wherever a web address is mentioned in the text it's indicated in red type – for example, **nationalarchives.gov.uk**. To avoid repetition, the **www.** that precedes the majority of addresses has, in most cases, been omitted. See right for more advice on accessing the websites given in this book.

GETTING STARTED ONLINE **51**

sections of a page. There are also options to download higher-quality images – these take longer to download, but you may be able to read the writing in the image more easily.

The Enhanced Image Viewer is designed to be used with the browser Internet Explorer, version 5.5 or later. It doesn't work with some other browsers, so you may need to switch to Internet Explorer to get the best out of the Ancestry site. To use the Enhanced Image Viewer, you'll need to install a special piece of browser software, or plug-in, on your computer (see page 40). Usually your computer will prompt you to install the plug-ins you need. If your browser settings or anti-virus software try to prevent installation, you'll find Ancestry's help pages have the information to solve the problem.

**Lawful union**
There's a double chance that you'll be able to trace your ancestors' wedding because most Anglican marriages generate two records: of the banns and of the marriage itself. In the 19th and early 20th centuries, weddings usually took place in the bride's parish church. Then, as now, the banns would be read by the vicar on three Sundays before the wedding. The banns publicly proclaim the couple's intention so help to avoid a bigamous or unlawful marriage. Records of banns and marriages can be found at **ancestry.co.uk**.

**DNA testing service**
Ancestry offers a range of DNA tests which allow you to find out if others with the same surname are related to you. You can buy a testing kit through the website and send off a simple mouth swab to get the results.

**Box tips** Many pages in the book include an information box offering extra research tips and advice relevant to the subject covered on that page. This might give you website addresses in **red type**, as well as actions that you'd need to carry out on your own computer.

## Using the case histories
You'll find your research supported by dozens of case histories showing step-by-step instructions on how to use websites to uncover information about your relatives. Many of these sites are free to use; others charge fees, although these will seem well worth it when your ancestors start to emerge.

Other case histories show you how to use national and regional archives, libraries and museums. And there are also step-by-step instructions to help you to create family trees on your computer, upload your results to the web and share your successes with family.

## When a website looks different
One of the things that makes the internet so exciting – and occasionally baffling – is that new websites and new information are constantly appearing. At the same time, established sites have closed down. The well-used **familyrecords.gov.uk**, for example, has closed since the last edition of this book. Even the established websites change their appearance. Just when you've become used to the look of a homepage, you'll open it up to find it looks different. Don't worry: it will still function in much the same way as it did before, as the principles involved in searching for information remain constant. If you find that the information search process has changed, the site will usually prompt you.

## When a web address won't work
Most internet sites require a prefix of **http://** and **www.** in front of the site name. However, in order to make the text in this book more readable, we've deleted most of these

prefixes. If you enter a website address as it's shown in the book, some browsers will automatically restore any missing prefixes. For those that don't, however, you must insert them for yourself. Unfortunately even this won't always work! Some websites are *not* designed with **www.** in the address, and will *not* function if it's included. Similarly, a small number of sites use unorthodox prefixes, such as **https://** or **www3**. In these cases – or for where an address has changed – enter the name of the site into Google or another search engine and you should be able to find the correct details.

best. Taking one step at a time helps you to avoid the common pitfalls that often beset newcomers to family research. Starting slowly and gradually going from success to success works best for most people.

present as possible. To get to your great grandparents, you first need to find out a much as you can about your grandparent Their life stories will contain clues that w make it much easier for you to find releva documentation about their parents.

**Advice from the experts**
Experienced family historians use the following research methods to ensure the best possible results.

**DON'T TAKE A GIANT LEAP BACKWARDS**
It's tempting to jump back to the 1901 ce and see if you can find anyone who migh

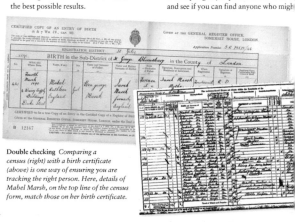

**Double checking** *Comparing a census (right) with a birth certificate (above) is one way of ensuring you are tracking the right person. Here, details of Mabel Marsh, on the top line of the census form, match those on her birth certificate.*

**As it was written** Where possible, the book shows you what the original records – such as a census return and birth certificate, above – look like. What you find online is often a transcription of a record, although you can often download and print off a copy of the original.

# Family history terms and abbreviations

**When you start to research your family's history, it's a good idea to get to know the sometimes unfamiliar words and phrases you'll come across. Some define family relationships and events, others crop up in documents and records.**

Being consistent right from the start in your use of terms and abbreviations will help you to avoid confusion farther along the line. It also means that other family historians will understand your notes if you publish your findings online. Using proper terminology when describing family relationships will help you to organise your family tree as you go and see at a glance how people are related.

## 'False' relatives

Most of us grew up calling all sorts of unrelated family friends and neighbours 'auntie' or 'uncle'. These honorary relatives need to be removed from the family tree to avoid confusion. Until quite recently, 'cousin' was often used as an all-purpose word for someone who is related to you but outside your immediate family. It's also easy to get confused with the terms 'half brother' (a brother through one parent only) and 'stepbrother' (a child of your step parent, unrelated to you).

## Describing family relationships

Working out the ways in which members of your family are related to one another isn't always easy. The relationships closest to you are usually fairly straightforward, but the farther back in time you go, the more complex they can become, particularly where there are divorces and remarriage. The chart on the right helps to clarify relationships.

### Common family history abbreviations

| | | | | | |
|---|---|---|---|---|---|
| b. | born | gf. | grandfather | s. and h. | son and heir |
| bach. | bachelor | gm. | grandmother | spin. | spinster |
| bapt. or bp. | baptised | ggf. | great grandfather | unm. | unmarried |
| bur. | buried | ggm. | great grandmother | w. | wife |
| by lic. | married by licence | inf. | infant | wdr. | widower |
| c. | christened | m. | married | wid. | widow |
| d. | died | mar. | married | 2. | second marriage |
| dau. | daughter | otp. | of this parish | = | married |
| dsp. | died childless | s. | son | ? | uncertain or unknown |

### Your own family relationships

This chart will help you to understand more complicated family relationships.

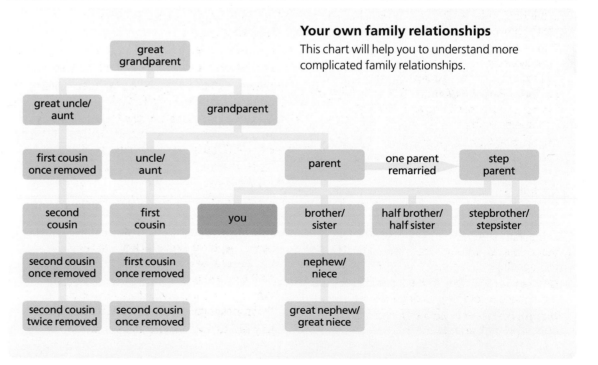

# Internet terms you need to know

**The introduction of the internet has created a flurry of new terms that you'll need to familiarise yourself with. They'll become a useful form of shorthand for your research.**

Like the internet itself, the terms that are used when you start researching your family history online continue to change and develop as people discover new ways of doing things. Keeping up with these new phrases can be challenging, but the words shown in the list here will make sure you start with the basics 'under your belt'. You may want to make a note of new phrases or acronyms that you come across.

## A glossary of internet terms

**Bandwidth** The capacity of your internet connection

**Bookmark** A facility to save links to favourite websites so that they're easy to find again

**Broadband** A means of connecting to the internet with a bigger bandwidth, which is faster than a dial-up connection

**Browser** A program for viewing web pages. In this book, Internet Explorer and Mozilla Firefox are the browsers used

**Cache** A directory on your computer that stores recently visited web pages so they can be loaded faster the next time you visit

**Cd-rom** Stands for Compact Disc Read Only Memory. A disc for storing and saving information from your PC

**Chat room** A website that allows you to take part in real time 'chat' conversations with other website users

**Cookie** Information sent by a website to be stored on your PC, which allows you to revisit a site and be signed in automatically

**Database** A structured collection of information that's stored on a computer, or a program to manage this sort of data

**Dataset** Another word for database, mainly used for digitised records from a single original source

**Dial-up connection** Connection to the internet using a phone line and a modem

**Download** Saving and storing information to your computer from the internet or another computer

**Email** Electronic mail, a method of communicating via the internet

**FAQ** Stands for Frequently Asked Questions, usually found on website help pages

**File** Information stored on your computer, created by you, which has been dated, stored and named

**Firewall** A filter to prevent unauthorised access to your computer from the internet

**Forum** A place on a website where visitors can post messages and share information

**Gateway** Usually relates to websites that are a source of information and links to internet resources on a particular topic

**Gedcom** Stands for GENealogical Data COMmunication. A standard file format for sharing family trees between different computers or programs

**Html** Stands for Hypertext Mark-up Language, the way in which a web page tells the browser how to display material on the web page

**ISP** Internet Service Provider – the company that supplies your internet connection

**Log off** To disconnect from a website

**Log on** To identify yourself to a website to gain access to its content or to facilities specifically intended for you

**Network** A series of computers, all connected so people can work together and share files

**Online** Connected to or located on the internet

**Password** A secret word that allows only a specific person to access certain internet resources

**Portal** A site that offers a single entry point for a selection of internet resources

**Search engine** A website that allows you to search for other websites by using key words; also a similar facility which searches an index of a single website

**Service provider** The company that supplies your internet service

**Software** Computer programs that can be installed on your computer to allow you to carry out certain tasks

**Spam** Junk email sent to large numbers of email addresses at once

**URL** Stands for Uniform Resource Locator – the unique web address for a web page

**Webmaster** The person who runs a website

**Website** A group of web pages in the same location

# First steps

Exploring your family's history is a wonderful adventure. Beginning with your living relatives and any old photographs or documents you can find, you can embark on a journey into the past that will enable you to discover your ancestry and create your family tree. This chapter introduces you to the many resources available to help you.

# What is family history?

**Your aim may be to draw up a family tree filled with your ancestors. But family history is so much more than that – an enthralling voyage of discovery, back through time, to discover what shaped you.**

The growth of the internet and the popularity of television programmes about family history have sparked off huge interest in finding out more about our past. The sense of achievement in tracing our ancestors has added to the appeal of this enthralling hobby, and more and more people are motivated by the desire to create a legacy to pass on to their children and grandchildren.

## Where did it all start?

In early medieval times, fighting knights adopted distinctive symbols, representing their family, to identify themselves. These were displayed on shields and on a surcoat worn over armour: the word 'surcoat' is the origin of 'coat' as in 'coat of arms'. At this time, only the nobility had coats of arms.

**Modern times**
*The arms granted to Dr Norman McIver in 2006 reflect his working life. His service as a Ghurka is represented by the kukri or short sword in the boar's mouth, while the red of the shield indicates a career in finance.*

By the late 13th century, lesser nobility and gentlemen had also started to adopt coats of arms. A specific coat of arms was passed down through the male line of the family, but important marriages were recognised by the inclusion of some of the symbols used by the bride's family, so that new emblems evolved. A daughter was entitled to inherit the family coat of arms intact only if the owner – or 'armiger' – died without a male heir.

**Family links** *Not only does a family share its genes, but it has a vast, shared history, too. Careful questioning will provide vital links.*

In 1530, Henry VIII sent heralds throughout England and Wales to register each coat of arms. Every family using one had to justify its claim through genealogical tables and proofs.

As a result of these investigations – or 'heraldic visitations' – many people had to give up their coats of arms when they couldn't prove their link to nobility. The regularity of

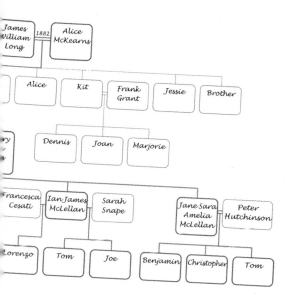

the visitations resulted in a wealth of records, mainly in the form of pedigrees – simple, linear family trees going back three to five generations from the time of compilation. The earliest genealogists were members of wealthy or noble families trying to establish the family's right to coats of arms, by tracing their forebears through heraldic records and thus proving their noble ancestry.

Today, these records are held by the College of Arms in London (see Directory), where royal heralds continue to check claims and issue new coats of arms. There may be a number of coats of arms for any one family, as coats were attached to individuals, not to surnames.

## The internet makes it so easy

Until the 1990s, family history research involved visiting local, county and national record offices to trawl through records.

Now, with the ease and speed of the internet, it's all so much faster. The internet has chat rooms where you can swap hints and tips, get advice if you are stuck, and where people will share their stories – especially if they discover a link to your family. Message boards are an excellent place to meet people to discuss your findings; you'll find a good selection if you key 'family history message boards' into Google.

Not everything is available online yet – you may still have to visit some record offices – but the advantage is that many of them have exhibitions and displays which may help to bring the past to life for you.

## Two routes to choose from

When you decide to start tracing your family's history, there are two main areas you can focus on. One is building a family tree and peopling it with as many ancestors as you can find. The other involves investigating a particular story, or ancestor, in detail.
● To begin with, most people choose the family tree route, because it gives you an overview of your family. The obvious starting point is your paternal line – you probably share the same surname and can track it back into the past. This might be quite straightforward if you have an unusual name.
● If your name is more common – Jones, Smith, MacDonald or Murphy, for example – it might be easier to start several lines of enquiry at once. This way, you'll find as many direct ancestors as possible. Remember that the number of people to think about and trace doubles each time you work back a generation – you have four grandparents,

eight great grandparents, 16 great great grandparents, and an impressive 32 great great great grandparents.

Searching through so many generations doesn't have to be daunting, if you start with what you already know – your immediate living family. Start by asking your parents and grandparents, uncles and aunts to tell you what they remember. If they're no longer alive, it's possible you may already have – or can get access to – family documents that will point you in the right direction.

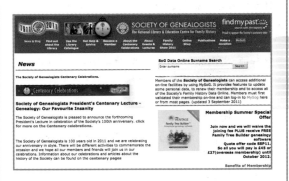

# Ten sites to get you started

**There are hundreds of websites for family historians, but here are ten that are particularly useful as they're easy to use and packed with information – just what you need for your online adventure.**

Some of these sites offer good basic information for beginners, others give you useful links to family history material on the web. There are sites to help you to find distant relatives, and sites with the historical information you'll need to build up a picture of your ancestors' lives.

There are, of course, hundreds of other key resources, many of which will be discussed within this book, but these ten represent the wide range of sites you may want to visit. They'll give you an idea of the astonishing amount of material that's available on the web.

**A family business**

Jewish immigrant Lazar Atlas, with his children Minnie and Maurice, stands in front of his grocery shop in Cheetham, Manchester, in the 1890s. If your ancestors owned a shop in a town or city their names and addresses – perhaps even their ages – would have been recorded regularly in official documents such as tax records and local business directories. These records can be accessed through the sites on the following pages, and may give a good insight into the business successes (or otherwise) of previous generations of your family.

# Great websites to begin your search

Most of these sites are free to use and will give you a good idea of the wealth of information available to you online.

## bbc.co.uk/familyhistory

Visit BBC Family History for top tips on getting started. Its content is linked to the television series *Who Do You Think You Are?* and the site provides a list of useful links to other organisations. There are also lively message boards where you can exchange information with other family historians.

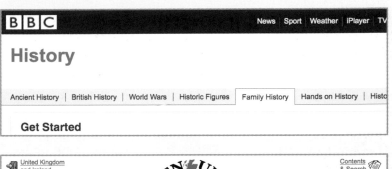

## genuki.org.uk

Genuki is designed to serve as a 'virtual reference library' of family history relevant to the UK and the Republic of Ireland. It's run by volunteers, and there are comprehensive sections devoted to every part of the British Isles, with details of record offices and links to online material. For many counties, there are even pages for individual towns and parishes (see page 44).

## cyndislist.com

Cyndi's List is a comprehensive site that has links to more than 200,000 online resources. Although maintained in the USA, Cyndi's List has a strong international section that includes the UK and the Republic of Ireland (see page 46).

## direct.gov.uk/gro

The General Register Office for England and Wales provides useful information on starting a family tree with birth, marriage and death certificates from 1 July 1837 onwards. It explains the information that is provided by these certificates and how to order and pay for them (see page 42).

## nationalarchives.gov.uk

The National Archives is the home of Britain's historical records. Its extensive website has material for everyone from the novice to the expert. There are basic guides to all the main national records of interest to family historians, and it's an essential site for anyone with ancestors in the army or navy. There's an online catalogue, and directories of both local record offices and the archives that those offices hold.

## rootsweb.com

RootsWeb is one of the oldest genealogy sites on the web. Its main value is as the home of thousands of family history mailing lists and message boards, devoted to places, surnames, occupations and other useful topics. Its WorldConnect service allows you to put your family tree online free of charge, and it has a good range of guides for beginners.

## ancestry.co.uk

For an annual subscription fee, Ancestry provides access to its expanding worldwide collection of records and indexes. Its databases include census returns, birth, marriage and death indexes, Irish and UK probate records, old telephone directories, military service papers, passenger lists and arrival records for the Port of New York (see page 50).

## findmypast.co.uk

Findmypast is a rich source of information for family historians looking for English and Welsh records. It holds indexes for civil registration and census returns, military indexes – particularly for the First World War – and migration records, which include passport applications and ships' passenger lists. There's also a wide range of occupational records. For more about the website, see page 52.

## Tracing rural records

A husband and wife labouring in fields might seem impossible to trace, but if they were tenant farmers or workers on the estate of a landowner, the records of their tenancy and the rent they paid may be shown in the estate archives. If the estate has remained in the same family, the archives may still be with them, but often they have been deposited in county record offices. Other useful resources include census records and some school archives, which may hold details of pupils' parents. You'll find links to county record offices and archives on websites such as Genuki and The National Archives.

## familysearch.org

Almost all the sites with large data collections are commercial and require payment. But FamilySearch is run by the Church of Jesus Christ of Latter-day Saints (the Mormons) and is free of charge. It has an index to the 1881 census of England and Wales, and millions of baptismal entries from parish registers. The Mormons have ambitious plans to add images to the site and millions more data entries (see page 54).

## genesreunited.co.uk

GenesReunited is one of the most popular UK sites for family historians. Anyone can upload a family tree for other users to see, and the aim is to help you to find people whose ancestors match yours. You need to register (which is free) to use it, and other people will be able to contact you. But to initiate contact with someone who has put their tree on the site, you'll need to pay the modest subscription (see page 272).

# Gathering information

The best place to start researching your family's past is with some careful offline detective work. Then you'll be ready to tap into the amazing resources of the internet.

# Start your search offline

**You may be surprised by how much you can find out about your relatives even before you venture online. Pulling together this information is vital preparation for the journey further into your family's past.**

*Picture clues Notes on photographs can provide important family history clues. Here, they reveal that William Wilcox of Fairford (right) was a handyman. The cottage that he and his father rented can be seen in the background.*

First, write down everything you know about your family – starting with yourself. Then include all you know about your nearest relatives – your parents, siblings, uncles, aunts and grandparents. Include as much detail as you can, making an accurate list of the full names, and dates of birth, marriage and death (where applicable), for all the members of your immediate family.

Add additional data such as where people lived or worked, and how and when they moved around the country. There's a lot of geography involved in tracing your family history, as you'll discover when you begin looking at certificates and census returns, so invest in a good atlas or street map.

## Identifying the gaps

This isn't simply a fact-finding mission; you are also highlighting areas that need research. It's unlikely that you'll be given names and biographical detail on all eight ancestors from three generations back, so you'll need to expand on what you're told. This might mean talking to more distant relations, or finding official documents such as birth, marriage and death certificates or census returns.

**Family portrait** *A tenant farmer, Jacob Pady (left), with his wife and children in a 1900 photograph taken on his farm at Colyton in Devon.*

## Set yourself a goal

It's a good idea to set limits, because it's easy to lose your focus as you gather information. Define what you want to achieve, and your research won't get muddled or lose direction. Decide whether you want to concentrate on one strand – a particular ancestor or a specific story – or work back in time and discover relatives you know nothing about.

If you go for the latter, decide whether to work back in a linear fashion, from generation to generation focusing only on direct forebears, or perhaps to branch out sideways and find siblings and cousins.

Whether you choose to concentrate on one side of the family or complete the whole

## Using record sheets

One way of keeping information is by filling in record sheets, particularly if you're getting details from electronically held data sources. Good examples can be found on the BBC website **bbc.co.uk/familyhistory**. Download and print as many of these sheets as you need.

**BBC** FAMILY HISTORY

Sheet ............
Contd ............    First information sheet

| NAME | Relation to you |
|------|-----------------|
| Birth date/place | Death date/place |
| SPOUSE 1 | SPOUSE 2 |
| Name | |

picture, make sure you know exactly what you're looking for and why, every time you start a new search – online or off.

## Keeping records

Organise your findings right from the outset and take clear notes as you do your research. Keep track of the searches you've done, make a note of record offices you've visited and record each website that you search. This will save you wasting a lot of time – and some money – going over old ground.

## Organise the paperwork

Once you start building up photocopies, print-outs from websites, notes, photographs and duplicate certificates on different branches of the family or individual ancestors, you'll want to be able to access them quickly. Work out a system of storage folders that suits you. There's no 'correct' method: just be consistent in the way you organise information in each folder. You can then keep your folders in chronological order, or cross-reference them by name.

# Collecting family memories

**Your parents and grandparents are a living link to the past, so ask them to tell you about the family. They should be able to provide information about more distant relatives – people you may never even have met.**

Talking to your relatives is one of the most important ways of finding out about previous generations. Reminiscences will give you the facts – names, dates and places linked to your family. But just as importantly, they add colour. What were these people like? Are there family secrets to be discovered? See what you can find out about the individual characteristics, likes and dislikes, loves and tragedies, occupations and skills, hobbies and pastimes of your ancestors. Capturing this oral history is a vital process that will allow you to preserve and pass on information to the next generation.

You can't rush the early stages of gathering information: it takes time and tact. It also requires careful thought and planning beforehand. Use these guidelines to help you to interview your relatives.

## Set clear objectives
Before you talk to someone, think carefully about what you want to find out.
● What do you want to achieve from the interview?
● Do you want to talk about one particular ancestor, or do you want to collect some stories about a range of people?

You may achieve more if you focus on only one line of questioning at a time, otherwise you could confuse your subject.

## Write down some questions
A good way to start is to write down some prompting questions in advance. These will help you to maintain your focus and not get sidetracked during the interview.
● Make the questions clear and relevant.
● Focus, where possible, on concrete things to begin with – the person's full name, place and date of birth and where they grew up.

Answering these straightforward questions may 'warm up' a reluctant relative, who'll then decide to elaborate and give you much greater detail or perhaps feel more willing to talk about more sensitive subjects. If you're lucky, a line of questioning will trigger valuable memories.

## Record the interview
It's a good idea to record your talk – partly so that you have an accurate record, but also to ensure that you have something to pass on to future generations.
● You can use a simple notebook, but these days there's so much technology available that it would be a shame to miss the opportunity to create a fuller record.
● After obtaining the subject's permission, you could use a camcorder, tape recorder or digital camera. Capturing how the relative looked and sounded will add an enormous amount to the records you create.

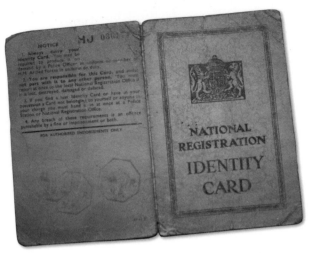

**Wartime ID** *During the Second World War, everyone, even children, had to carry an identity card like this one, giving the holder's age, occupation, marital status and home address.*

● Later, you might want to incorporate the interview onto your own website (see page 304), but do get permission before putting any personal material online.

## Be a good interviewer
Good interviewing techniques are essential. Relatives usually relish the chance to tell stories from their past – but not always, so try to be as sensitive as possible.
● Make sure your subject is relaxed and happy to tell their tale.
● Never push someone on a topic that they are clearly uncomfortable talking about. Respect their wishes if they don't want to talk. You may be able to find the missing information from someone else.
● Be patient, and offer to come back another time, if you sense your relative is tiring.

## Verify your facts

Although your relative may be adamant about a date of birth or a family story, don't accept everything you hear as fact. Memories can play tricks on elderly people, and some of what you hear may not be accurate.

• Take the information away and verify everything with official documents, as this will save you problems later.

• Try to compare versions of the same story as told by different relatives. Where accounts overlap, there's likely to be an element of truth. When they vary, do more research.

## False relatives and nicknames

Those aunties and uncles being referred to may not necessarily be blood relations. They could be longstanding friends that have earned honorary family status.

• Establish exactly who is a blood relative through official documentation.

• Make sure you find the full, given names, and check official documents, because pet names or nicknames used by the family can confuse your search. The youngest daughter in a family may have been nicknamed 'Dolly' by her sisters, because she was so much smaller than they were – but you won't find her under that name on any birth certificate.

## Starting from scratch

Even if you have no living relatives, you can still start creating your own family tree. Begin by looking at your own birth certificate. From this, you might be able to get an approximate date for your parents' marriage, which could lead you to their marriage certificate and details of their parents.

## Ten leading questions

Here are some questions you might ask close family members and elderly relatives. Some could release a wealth of memories and vital clues.

1 Will you give me your full name, your date of birth and where you were born, and the date and place of your marriage?

2 What can you tell me about your parents and grandparents? Do you know your grandmothers' maiden names?

3 Did anyone have a nickname?

4 Can you tell me anything about the jobs our ancestors did?

5 How did they look and what were they like? And have you got any photographs I could borrow?

6 Can you remember the house you grew up in? Or even the address?

7 What schools did the family attend? Did anyone go on to university – if so, which one?

8 Did the family go to church – if so, which one?

9 Do you have childhood memories of relatives? Are you sure they were blood relations?

10 Can you remember any family christenings, weddings or funerals?

Often, older people who've experienced traumatic events or difficult childhoods simply refuse to talk about the past. In such a case, you could try, with the utmost tact, to ask them to write down their memories and leave the pages to you in their will.

# Discovering the stuff of life

**Tracing your family history isn't just about dates and facts – it's also about the real, flesh-and-blood personalities in your family. Rummaging through family memorabilia can tell you a lot about them.**

When you look at photographs of your great grandparents or other ancestors, they may seem a little formal and staid. But behind those 'proper' appearances were real characters – brave, weak, adventurous or even totally outrageous. It's only through discovering the things they left behind, or sent to other people, that you start to get a fuller idea of them as human beings.

If you're lucky, your older relations will have a collection of memorabilia that can help you to build up a picture of your family – old football programmes, ration books, letters and so on. These are often kept in drawers or files, a scrapbook or a precious box of 'treasures', and are powerful clues.

**OFFICIAL PAPERS** Birth, marriage or death certificates are the most obvious starting point. Official documents will usually have clear, verifiable data on them. Find as many as possible, because not only will these help to confirm – or disprove – some of the information you've already been given, but they'll also save you

**Hidden treasures** *Memorabilia and documents such as letters, wills, medals and certificates are important in rounding out the realities behind the pictures. They tell the story of personalities and circumstances that the official records omit.*

time and money when it comes to buying certificates online. The last thing you want is to duplicate anything that already exists within the family.

**WILLS** Usually written near the time of death, wills give a snapshot not only of assets and funds, but also of family and friends. A will might tell you more about the person's most treasured possessions. It might mention land, a house or an occupation – or even reveal a long-hidden family secret.

**FAMILY BIBLE** If you're lucky enough to have a family Bible, it could hold information vital to your search, such as names and dates of former owners and their families. Look in the Bible for its year of publication – any information that precedes that date will have been written down from memory after the Bible was acquired, and needs to be verified.

**BITS AND PIECES** Printed ephemera, such as cinema tickets and theatre programmes, give an insight into the person's standard of living as well as their pastimes and hobbies. School reports are fascinating, as they show people in their formative years – through the eyes of their witty or acerbic teachers.

### Respect people's privacy

Remember that items of family memorabilia, and especially letters and postcards, can be extremely personal. They should never be taken or read without the express permission of the owner. You'll need to be sensitive and diplomatic in this area of your research.

## Serving their country

With two World Wars in the 20th century, as well as National Service, your ancestors may well have served in the military. This generates memorabilia such as service papers, medals – often giving details of regiments or ships that your ancestor served with – and uniform insignia. Keep a look out for other items, such as letters and postcards sent home while on active service, ration books and identity cards. It's a good idea to check whether any of your forebears kept diaries: these can give fascinating insights into wartime life, both at home and abroad. To deal with the shortage of manpower for the Army's peace-time commitments, National Service was started in 1949. Young men had to do 12 months' full-time service followed by five years' reserve service. It wasn't long before the 12 month period was extended to 18 months – and in 1950 it went up to two years. The last men were called up in 1960, and National Service finally ended in 1962.

# Finding clues in photos

**Family photographs are our windows on the past. If you're lucky, you may have one or two portraits dating from the 19th century. Family photo albums can help you to put faces to some of the names in your family tree.**

Go through photographs with your elderly relatives and ask them what they can remember about the picture – who's in it, and when and where it was taken. You may find the names of people in a photo or the date it was taken written on the back. This could involve removing a photo from its frame – which may uncover further hidden treasures, such as a newspaper cutting or a revealing letter.

**MAKE A COPY** If the picture's not yours, borrow it or take a digital shot and download it to your computer; then record any names that appear on the back. Once you've found a name or two, the missing names should fall into place.

**Tracing the studio** *The photographer's name and address can be useful research tools, particularly if written records survive.*

**STUDIO PHOTOS** Formal occasions were often captured by a local professional. If you can't recognise people or events in a photo, look for the address of the photographer's studio, as in the pictures shown below. You may be able to find the studio through old local trade directories (see pages 230-3) which could point to when and where the picture was taken. The studio's address might also suggest the area where these ancestors lived, as it was probably within walking distance.

**OUTDOOR PHOTOS** Cars, buses and buildings in the picture can help you to date or locate the shot. A house or street name may lead you to a family home, as might a photo taken at a local landmark, especially if you can link it to surviving family letters referring to an outing.

**FASHION OR 'SUNDAY BEST'?** Look at what the subjects are wearing. Your local archive, studies centre or museum, or even the Victoria and Albert Museum (see Directory), may be able to help you to date their clothing. Clothes can also cast light on your ancestors' social standing, but remember that people tended to dress up for a session at the photographer's and their 'Sunday best' could be 20 years out of date.

## Harness technology

Faded or damaged pictures can be restored at a photographic or print shop. Digitally scanning your photographs and uploading them onto your computer will allow you to embed them into an online family tree (see page 312), or email them to relatives who may be able to identify people and events.

**Military detail** *Puttees and the motorbike date this photo to the First World War. Badges, buttons and buckles, if visible, give useful clues. Military websites may be able to help you to identify a regiment (see page 192).*

## Preserve and protect

Keep precious photographs and documents away from heat, light and damp and, where possible, store them in sturdy boxes. You can buy containers designed for storing fragile memorabilia from **memories-nostalgia.com**.

Digital scrapbooking is another option. You can now create virtual photo albums that can be arranged page by page and printed out. There's a range of software available to help you to do this – from LumaPix FotoFusion at **lumapix.com**.

Other websites, such as Flickr (see page 318) and Nations Memorybank (see page 322), allow you to upload and organise your family photographs online.

## Clues in the background

Lots of old family photos are just informal snapshots of the family at home or enjoying a day out. You can often date these photographs – at least to the nearest decade – by looking carefully at background detail as well as what the subjects are wearing and doing.

In this picture, a number of clues tell you that it was probably taken in the 1930s. The chair could have been made in the early 20th century but it has obviously been re-covered and the ends of the arms look a little worn.

The fireplace is a Victorian register grate, a type first used after 1850, but the nursery fireguard is early 20th century. The fire-irons show that it was a working fireplace, typical of most homes until after the Second World War, and the sprigged wallpaper is typical of the period between 1910 and 1920.

Above the fireplace, a selection of photographs pinned to the wall could be of loved ones killed in the First World War. On the mantelpiece, a pocket watch could have belonged to a close family member.

When you look at your own photos, remember that pieces of furniture or grandfather clocks may predate the photo by decades. But other items such as lamps, radios and record players are likely to be contemporary and may be a recognisable and easily dated design. For help with dating items, see page 26.

# Period pieces

If you're lucky enough to find items from your family's past tucked away in an attic or drawer, or if you have keepsakes handed down from generation to generation, you may be able to make fascinating discoveries about your ancestors, their lives and their interests.

Uncovering the stories behind inherited objects is as enthralling as investigating the 'official' side of your ancestors' lives, and will open up a whole new area of research. So many items have a story to tell, from everyday articles such as toys, ceramics, pottery and silverware to more cherished possessions like jewellery, retirement clocks, prizes for sports achievement or a family bible.

## The way people looked

You may come across clothing that belonged to an ancestor, or military keepsakes such as medals or badges. These are valuable clues that can be dated, enabling you to find a regiment or identify a relative, as well as telling you something about their lifestyle. Even modern items are important: a pair of platform shoes, a mini-skirt or a silk chiffon evening gown will tell you that your relative followed the latest trends.

Old family photos yield clues, too, from clothes, locations or the type of event, such as a wedding or street party. Try your local museum for help on dating items in a photo, or the Victoria and Albert Museum (see box, right), or visit the

**Sharp dresser** *Finding a mini dress like this by Mary Quant from 1967 tells you that a relative kept up with the fashions.*

1860s  1880s  1890s

**Getting the picture** *If you find old photos but no dates, you might be able to place them by changes in fashion. In the first photo, the woman wears a full, wide dress popular in the 1860s. By the time of the next photo, in the 1880s, dresses were more fitted with tight high-necked bodices, while the final picture shows the wide-brimmed hat popular towards the end of the 19th century.*

'Date an old photograph' pages on **cartes.freeuk.com/**. For military photos, watch for cap badges, ranking insignia and regimental crests.

Jewellery that has been handed down from generation to generation may have more than just sentimental value. Silver can be identified through its hallmark, and many marks are listed online. The Silvermine website at **freespace.virgin.net/a.data/** will help.

## Treasures in the home

Most families have collected some ceramic pieces over time. There's usually information on the base of plates or other items that you can use to either date the piece, or work out the name of the potter or factory. If it's a small, local company, you can start to narrow down where your ancestors might have lived. Websites to help you to date and identify ceramics include the International Ceramic Directory (see box, right).

Toys that have been treasured and handed down over the years also shed light on the childhoods of our ancestors. Those from recent decades are easiest to place, but you may find older toys that could be dated. A hollow-cast lead soldier, for instance, might be marked 'William Britain',

**Boys' toys** *If you find Dinky toys, they're quite likely to date from the 1950s (right), when they became a huge craze for Britain's boys.*

**Packaging clues** *Even a container can be revealing. The Huntley & Palmer's biscuit tin from 1900, left, shows five scenes of Navy life.*

a British company that started making such figures in 1893. They all stand on a flat base and those made before 1912 are marked simply 'William Britain'. After 1912, 'Ltd.' was included with the name, and after 1917 'England' was added.

You may also find dolls or teddy bears packed away. Many dolls are marked on the back of the neck, below the hairline, with the manufacturer's stamp, which helps to identify both maker and date. The Museum of Childhood (see box, right) has more than 8,000 dolls in its collection, and the website may help you to date any that you find.

## Counting the time

Clocks, watches or other memorabilia presented at retirement or on another occasion can provide valuable information about an ancestor. Look for an inscription that might say when your relative received the gift, the company or organisation he worked for, his period of service and the position he held.

If there's no inscription, the style of watch can tell you much: a hunter pocket watch (with a cover) or half-hunter (with a window in the cover) were popular in the mid to late 19th century and could reveal an interest in country pursuits. Wrist watches came to the fore during the First World War, as the most practical kind of timepiece for use in the trenches. Then, as the popularity of motoring spread from the 1920s, curved watches, known as drivers' watches, became fashionable – the driver could still read the face with both hands on the steering wheel.

**Show time** *Before the wrist watch there was the pocket watch. The example below, from around 1900, has an open glass face, which meant its use was at least partly decorative.*

## Websites to use for dating objects

The following organisations and websites can help you to identify and date the memorabilia you find, adding colour and interest to the ancestors on your family tree.

**Angels costumiers fancydress.com**
A costume-hire company that supplies costumes for films and museums as well as to the general public. A look around their website can help you to date period clothing.

**Victoria and Albert Museum vam.ac.uk**
The London museum is a great resource for clothing, jewellery and antiques. A visit to the website can get you started dating your fashions and other memorabilia.

**Museum of Childhood vam.ac.uk/moc** Part of the Victoria and Albert museum, the Museum of Childhood has a wide range of all kinds of toys through the ages, including dolls, teddy bears and games.

**International Ceramic Directory ceramic-link.de** Pottery and porcelain marks from all over their world can be seen and checked on the website. Use it to help you to identify your finds.

**National Maritime Museum nmm.ac.uk**
The museum has a large collection of jewellery dating from the 16th to early 20th centuries, including buckles, broaches, rings and watches. It can help you to find out more about the objects in your collection that have an 'official' or 'maritime' look.

**Imperial War Museum iwm.org.uk**
The website (see also page 195) includes a large collection of medals and other war-related objects. It has pictures and information that help you not only to identify medals, but also to find when and why they were awarded.

# Secrets of successful research

**When you begin investigating your family history, it's tempting to dive into the first website or record office you come across, to see what you can find. Wait, follow these simple guidelines and you'll be far more successful.**

It may not sound thrilling, but you'll find a methodical approach to family history is best. Taking one step at a time helps you to avoid the common pitfalls that often beset newcomers to family research. Starting slowly and gradually going from success to success works best for most people.

## Advice from the experts

Experienced family historians use the following research methods to ensure the best possible results.

**WORK BACK IN TIME** Go back through the generations, starting from as close to the present as possible. To get to your great grandparents, you first need to find out as much as you can about your grandparents. Their life stories will contain clues that will make it much easier for you to find relevant documentation about their parents.

**DON'T TAKE A GIANT LEAP BACKWARDS**

It's tempting to jump back to the 1911 census and see if you can find anyone who might be a relative. Unless you have researched and identified actual family members in a precise location, you're likely to be disappointed. You may have to pay for some searches to be done, so it would be a waste of money to go after certificates of people who might not be related to you at all.

**WORK FROM KNOWN FACT TO KNOWN FACT**

If you come across a gap in the trail leading back to an ancestor, don't assume a link. Instead, try to find some supporting evidence from another source. If you can't find any evidence, you'll be unable to prove that particular connection conclusively, which means that any work you do beyond this point will be based on supposition – and will be tainted with an element of doubt. Come back to it later, when you've found evidence.

**QUESTION OFFICIAL DATA** Family historians rely heavily on official sources such as civil registration certificates for births, marriages and deaths; census records; parish register entries and wills. But this data is only as accurate as the person recording or providing it – and some of your ancestors might have given false information for a variety of personal reasons. An example is the census: these were taken every ten years, but when people's stated ages are compared over the decades, the age gaps often don't add up. Where possible, find at least two different sources that give the same details; that way there's more chance of the 'facts' being true.

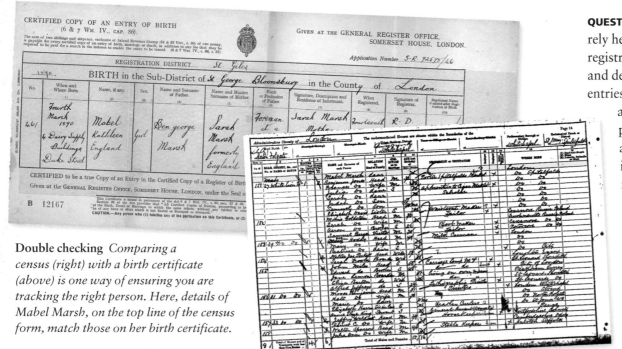

**Double checking** *Comparing a census (right) with a birth certificate (above) is one way of ensuring you are tracking the right person. Here, details of Mabel Marsh, on the top line of the census form, match those on her birth certificate.*

**BE WARY OF ONLINE DATA** Information that appears on the internet isn't always true. Errors can creep into any transcribed information, so don't take it as an indisputable fact – verify it by looking on at least one other website.

**CHECK THE ORIGINAL SOURCES**
Individuals who put data online don't always cite the original source of the information they've uploaded onto their website. But if they do, make a habit of verifying it offline, to ensure that it has been transcribed or used in the right way. You certainly don't want to incorporate someone else's mistakes into your own work.

**SEE IF THE FACTS REALLY FIT** Resist importing data into your own findings unless you're sure there's a link. It's tempting to link into a family tree you've found online when the facts appear to fit. Stick to the rule of working back in time until you've reached the relevant period, and then see if the facts still fit – remembering to double check the sources offline, too.

**ASK PERMISSION** If you want to incorporate someone else's research work into your own, contact them to ask permission first; many sites are protected by personal copyright. At the very least, you can use this process to check the accuracy of the information by asking questions about their research. If you do use someone else's work, be sure to credit them for their contribution, by showing their internet address properly when you incorporate their data.

## Family history in miniature

The practice of having miniature portraits painted was the early equivalent of the studio photograph. Here, a family is able to view the changing generations through painted portraits, bringing it up to date with personal photographs. In the first portrait, Thomas Offspring Blackall is wearing a uniform that could be from Harrow School, so that would be a good place to start searching for his records.

*Thomas Offspring Blackall 1832-79*

*Anne Phoebe Meeres 1867-1954*

*Kathleen Ruth McColl 1903-66*

*Anne Christina Snape 1928-*

*Virginia Mary Snape 1955-*

*Phoebe Snape 1990-*

# Keeping a record

**It's tempting to plunge in and start pulling together all sorts of random information, but if you're to avoid wasting time and effort by going over old ground, good record keeping is essential.**

Take some time to think about how you're going to organise your material right from the start. Whether you're working offline or online, making a note of previous searches avoids time-wasting duplication and helps you to remember exactly where you are with your research. It should prompt you to re-check material after a new discovery or return to areas of work that you deliberately left for another day.

## Offline searches

Where records haven't been digitised, you will need to carry out your searches at libraries or archives. Make a note of the document reference for each item you have viewed, the archive in which you found it and the date you examined the document. Write down the page number of any item you quote from or copy. Don't forget that each archive will have its own reference system. If you make any changes to your notes and files, remember to mark down the date and the reason for the amendment.

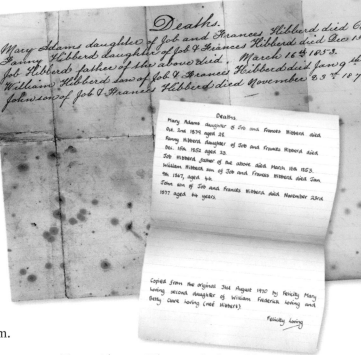

**Treat with care** *When you find an old, rather fragile document packed with information, make a transcript of all the details and then work from that, rather than risk damaging the old document with too frequent handling.*

**Gather your resources** *Ask an older member of the family to go through all the material you have collected so far. Write down any information they can give you and note the areas that will need further research.*

## Online searches

Make a list of all the websites that you've visited, and the indexes that you've searched, as you go along. If you don't take this basic step it's all too easy to forget which sites you've seen, and what you've examined when you were there. At the same time, make a list of the pages you've browsed. You can copy and paste these from your browser into a document for filing electronically, or you can print the pages out and store them with any offline records you've collected. Update this record after each set of searches.